guided by the lamp

The Story of Florence Nightingale for Kids

sarah michaels

contents

1 /

the early years

IMAGINE LIVING IN THE 1800S, a time when many people didn't think women should work outside the home, especially not in hospitals. Hospitals back then were often dirty and over-crowded places where people went when they had no other options. Being a nurse was not a respected job. In fact, it was usually a job for people who couldn't find other work. Nurses weren't trained like they are today, and the conditions in hospitals were often so bad that going to one could make you sicker instead of better.

But Florence Nightingale saw things differently. Born into a wealthy family in 1820 in Florence, Italy (that's where her name comes from!), she was expected to grow up, get married, and live a comfortable life. Her family didn't think it was proper for a lady to work, especially not in a hospital. But from a young age, Florence felt that she was meant to do something more. She believed that helping people, especially those who were sick, was one of the most important things a person could do.

Florence wasn't like other girls her age. While many girls were interested in dresses, parties, and finding a good husband, Florence spent her time reading books about science, medicine, and statistics. She loved learning about how the human body worked and what made people sick. She was especially interested in how to make sick people better. Even as a child, Florence would spend time taking care of sick animals or helping the poor people in her village. She knew that she was meant to help others, even if it meant going against what everyone else thought she should do.

When Florence was a young woman, she made a decision that shocked her family: she wanted to become a nurse. At the time, this was almost unheard of for someone of her social standing. Her family was horrified. They didn't think nursing was a job for a lady, especially one from a wealthy family. But Florence was determined. She knew that nursing was her calling, and she wasn't going to let anything stop her from following it.

Florence's determination led her to study nursing in secret, reading medical books and learning everything she could about how to care for the sick. She visited hospitals to learn more about how they worked and what could be done to make them better. Over time, she became convinced that the way hospitals were run needed to change. She believed that with better hygiene, organization, and care, hospitals could be places where people went to get well, not places where they went because they had no other choice.

Her chance to make a difference came during the Crimean War, which started in 1853. This was a war fought between several countries, including Britain, where Florence lived. Thousands of British soldiers were sent to fight in a place far from home, and many of them ended up in hospitals because of the terrible conditions on the battlefield. The hospitals were overcrowded, dirty, and poorly managed. Many soldiers died not from their wounds but from infections and diseases they caught while in the hospital.

When news of the terrible conditions reached Britain, people were outraged. They demanded that something be done to help the soldiers. Florence Nightingale was asked to lead a group of nurses to the war zone to help improve the conditions in the hospitals. This was a huge responsibility, but Florence was ready for the challenge.

When she arrived at the hospital in Scutari, what she found was worse than she could have imagined. The hospital was filthy, with dirt and grime everywhere. The beds were packed tightly together, and there were no proper toilets or places for the soldiers to wash. Rats and insects were everywhere, and the smell was awful. Many of the soldiers were dying from diseases like cholera and typhoid fever, which spread quickly in such dirty conditions.

Florence knew that things had to change, and fast. She got to work immediately, organizing the nurses and making a plan to clean up the hospital. She made sure that the soldiers had clean beds, proper food, and fresh water. She insisted that the floors be scrubbed, and that everything be kept as clean as possible. She even wrote letters back home asking for supplies and money to help make the hospital better.

But Florence didn't just stop at cleaning up the hospital. She also took care of the soldiers in a way that no one had before. She made sure that they were not just treated for their injuries, but that they were cared for as people. She listened to their stories, comforted them when they were scared or in pain, and made sure that they knew someone cared about them. Every night, she would walk through the hospital with a lamp, checking on each soldier to make sure they were comfortable and had everything they needed. This is how she became known as "The Lady with the Lamp."

Florence's work in the Crimean War was just the beginning of her impact on the world. When she returned to Britain after the war, she was a national hero. People everywhere admired her courage and dedication. But Florence wasn't interested in fame. She was more interested in making sure that what she had learned in the war could be used to help others.

She wrote books and reports on how hospitals should be run, using her experience in the Crimean War to show what worked and what didn't. She argued that hospitals needed to be clean, well-organized, and focused on the well-being of the patients. She also believed that nurses needed to be properly trained and educated, so they could provide the best care possible. Because of her work, nursing became a respected profession, and hospitals began to change for the better.

Florence didn't stop there. She also worked to improve healthcare for all people, not just soldiers. She believed that everyone, no matter how rich or poor, deserved to be cared for when they were sick. She set up the first school for nurses, where women could learn the skills they needed to be great nurses. She also worked on improving public health, focusing on things like clean water, proper sewage systems, and good nutrition.

Florence Nightingale's ideas were revolutionary, and they changed the way people thought about healthcare. Because of her, hospitals became places where people went to get better, and nursing became a profession that people respected. Her work saved countless lives, not just during the Crimean War, but in the years and decades that followed..

florence's childhood

Florence Nightingale's story begins long before she became the "Lady with the Lamp." To understand how she grew into the person who changed nursing forever, it helps to look back at her childhood. Florence was born on May 12, 1820, into a world of wealth and privilege. Her family was part of the upper class, and they lived in a big, beautiful house in the English countryside. But even though Florence had everything she could ever want, she was different from most children her age. Instead of being interested in fancy clothes, parties, and social events, Florence was curious about the world around her and was driven by a deep desire to help others.

Growing up in a wealthy family meant that Florence had access to the best education available at the time. This was unusual for a girl in the 1800s, as most girls were not encouraged to study subjects like math and science. But Florence's parents, William and Frances Nightingale, believed in educating their daughters. They hired private tutors who taught Florence and her older sister, Parthenope, a wide range of subjects. Florence excelled in her studies, showing a particular talent for mathematics, which was quite rare for girls during that period.

But it wasn't just her academic skills that set Florence apart. From a very young age, she displayed a deep compassion for living creatures. Florence loved animals, and her home was filled with them—dogs, cats, horses, and even a pet owl named Athena, which she found injured and nursed back to health. Florence took her responsibility to care for animals seriously, often spending hours making sure they were fed, comfortable, and happy. This love for animals was a sign of the deep empathy that would later define her work with people.

Florence's compassion wasn't limited to animals. Even as a child, she was drawn to helping those who were less fortunate. While other children might have been content to play games and enjoy their toys, Florence felt a strong sense of duty to care for others. She would often visit the poor and sick people in her village, bringing them food, medicine, and comfort. These visits were not just about giving charity; they were about understanding people's needs and figuring out how to make their lives better. Florence was deeply moved by the suffering she saw, and she began to think about how she could make a real difference in the world.

One story from Florence's childhood shows just how strong her sense of duty was, even at a young age. When she was about seven years old, she found a wounded dog near her home. Most children would have been afraid to approach the animal, but not Florence. She gently picked up the dog, brought it home, and tended to its injuries. Florence didn't stop there. She made sure the dog had a comfortable place to sleep and enough food and water. She watched over it until it was fully healed. This experience, along with many others, reinforced her belief that caring for those who were suffering—whether they were animals or people—was the most important thing she could do with her life.

Florence's early education wasn't just about learning facts and figures; it was also about developing her character. Her parents encouraged her to think deeply about the world around her and to question the things she didn't understand. They exposed her to different ideas and philosophies, allowing her to form her own opinions. Florence's father, William, was particularly influential in this regard. He was a well-educated man who believed in the power of knowledge. He often discussed complex ideas with Florence, treating her as an intellectual equal despite her young age. This approach to education helped Florence develop a strong mind and a clear sense of purpose.

As she grew older, Florence became more aware of the expectations society had for her. In the 1800s, girls from wealthy families were expected to focus on finding a good husband, raising children, and managing a household. But Florence wasn't interested in this traditional path. She knew that her calling was to help others, and she wasn't willing to let society's expectations stand in her way. This determination sometimes caused friction within her family, especially with her mother, who wanted Florence to follow a more conventional life.

Despite the pressure to conform, Florence remained true to herself. She spent her teenage years studying even more intensely, focusing on subjects that would later help her in her nursing career, such as anatomy, public health, and hospital administration. She also continued her visits to the poor and sick, learning more about the conditions they lived in and the challenges they faced. These experiences deepened her understanding of the suffering in the world and strengthened her resolve to do something about it.

Florence's love for animals and her desire to help others were not just hobbies; they were the foundations of her character. These qualities would later become the driving force behind her work in nursing. She saw every life, whether human or animal, as valuable and deserving of care and respect. This belief guided her actions throughout her life and shaped the way she approached her work.

One of the most important aspects of Florence's childhood was the way her parents nurtured her sense of independence. Although they didn't always agree with her choices, they respected her intelligence and her passion for helping others.

This support allowed Florence to explore her interests and develop the skills she would later use to revolutionize nursing. Her parents might not have understood why Florence was so determined to become a nurse, but they recognized that she was driven by something larger than herself.

Florence's childhood was also marked by a strong sense of spirituality. She believed that her desire to help others was a calling from God, and this belief gave her the strength to pursue her goals despite the obstacles in her way. Florence's faith was a source of comfort and guidance throughout her life, and it played a crucial role in shaping her worldview. She believed that every person had a purpose, and that hers was to care for the sick and suffering.

As Florence grew into a young woman, her determination to follow her calling only became stronger. She continued to educate herself, seeking out opportunities to learn more about medicine and healthcare. She read medical journals, studied hospital reports, and even visited hospitals to see firsthand how they were run. Florence was not content to sit back and wait for someone else to make the changes she wanted to see in the world. She was determined to be the one to make those changes herself.

a strong-willed girl

One story that really shows Florence's determination happened when she was about ten years old. At the time, Florence's family had a big garden with lots of beautiful flowers, trees, and shrubs. Florence loved spending time in the garden, not just because of the flowers but because it was a place where she could observe the birds, insects, and other animals that lived there. One day, she noticed that some of the plants were wilting and dying. The gardener told her it was because of a lack of water, and that there wasn't much they could do because the summer had been so dry.

Most children would have accepted this explanation and moved on to play with something else. But not Florence. She wasn't content to just watch the plants die. She started thinking about how she could save them. After observing the garden for a few days, she noticed that some areas got more shade than others, which meant they didn't dry out as quickly. She also realized that some plants needed more water than others.

With this information in mind, Florence came up with a plan. She gathered all the buckets and containers she could find and began collecting water from the house, the nearby stream, and even rain barrels. Then, she carefully watered the plants that needed it most, making sure to give them just enough water without wasting any. She even moved some of the more delicate plants to shadier spots where they would be protected from the harsh sun.

This might not sound like a big deal, but it was a huge task for a ten-year-old girl, especially considering that she did it all on her own. Her determination paid off, and many of the plants that had been wilting began to recover. The gardener was amazed, and Florence's parents were proud of her initiative. But more than anything, this story shows how Florence was able to take a problem, analyze it, and come up with a solution—something that would become a hallmark of her life and work.

Another example of Florence's strong will can be seen in how she dealt with her education. As you already know, Florence loved to learn, and she was particularly interested in subjects like math and science. However, in the 1800s, it wasn't considered proper for girls to study these subjects. Girls were expected to focus on things like music, art, and sewing—skills that would help them run a household and be good wives. But Florence didn't care about what was considered proper. She was fascinated by math, especially statistics, and she wanted to learn as much as she could.

Florence's father, William Nightingale, supported her interest in math and science. He provided her with books and tutors, and he encouraged her to pursue her studies. But not everyone in Florence's life was as supportive. Her mother, Frances, was concerned that Florence's interest in these "unladylike" subjects would make it difficult for her to find a suitable husband. Frances tried to steer Florence toward more traditional activities, but Florence wouldn't be swayed. She knew what she wanted to learn, and she wasn't going to let anyone stop her.

One day, when Florence was about twelve years old, her mother invited some friends over for tea. These friends had daughters around Florence's age, and Frances hoped that Florence would spend time with them, playing the piano or doing embroidery —activities that were considered appropriate for young ladies. But when the guests arrived, Florence was nowhere to be found. Her mother searched the house, growing more and more frustrated, until she finally found Florence in the library, deeply engrossed in a book on mathematics.

Frances was upset, but Florence calmly explained that she was working on a particularly difficult problem and that she would join the guests as soon as she was finished. Florence's mother tried to insist that she come right away, but Florence was firm. She wasn't being disrespectful—she simply believed that her studies were important, and she didn't see why she should have to stop just because guests had arrived. Eventually, her mother relented, and Florence was able to finish her work before joining the others.

This incident might seem small, but it highlights something important about Florence's character. She wasn't afraid to stand up for what she believed in, even if it meant going against the expectations of those around her. This strong will would later help her challenge the way hospitals were run and push for reforms that would save countless lives.

Florence's determination wasn't just limited to her studies and her garden. She was also fiercely independent in her thinking. While other girls her age were content to accept what they were told, Florence always asked questions and sought out answers for herself. She wanted to understand the world around her, and she wasn't satisfied with easy or superficial explanations.

One example of this independence of thought happened when Florence was about fourteen years old. Her family was visiting some relatives, and one evening, the adults were having a discussion about the role of women in society. Most of the adults believed that women should focus on their roles as wives and mothers, and that they didn't need to worry about things like politics or education. Florence listened quietly for a while, but eventually, she couldn't stay silent any longer.

She spoke up, arguing that women were just as capable as men and that they should have the same opportunities for education and careers. The adults were shocked—this was not the kind of opinion they expected from a fourteen-year-old girl, especially one from a wealthy family. But Florence didn't back down. She calmly and logically explained her point of view, using examples from history and literature to support her arguments.

Although the adults didn't all agree with her, they couldn't help but be impressed by her intelligence and conviction. This was a defining moment for Florence, as it was one of the first times she openly challenged the status quo. It also showed that even at a young age, she had the courage to speak out for what she believed in, even when it wasn't popular.

2 /
the calling

the voice of destiny

FLORENCE NIGHTINGALE GREW up in a world that had very specific ideas about what a girl's life should look like. For someone from a wealthy family like hers, the future was supposed to be predictable: learning the skills needed to run a household, attending social events, and eventually marrying a suitable husband. But Florence didn't see herself in this kind of future. From a very young age, she felt something inside her that she couldn't quite explain—a sense that she was meant to do something important, something different. It was as if a voice deep inside her was calling her to a purpose that went beyond the expectations of society.

Florence first began to hear this "voice of destiny" when she was still a child. She wasn't like other girls who dreamed of balls and beautiful dresses. Instead, Florence dreamed of helping people, especially those who were suffering. This wasn't just a passing interest for her; it was something she felt in her heart every day. When she looked around and saw people in need, she couldn't just walk away. It was as if she was being pulled toward them, compelled to find a way to help.

As Florence got older, this feeling only grew stronger. She began to realize that the calling she felt was to become a nurse, a profession that, at the time, was not respected or encouraged, especially for someone of her social standing. Nurses were often seen as untrained and unskilled, and the work they did was considered dirty and unworthy of a lady. But none of this mattered to Florence. She didn't care about the status or the opinions of others. She just knew, deep in her soul, that this was what she was meant to do.

It wasn't easy for Florence to accept this calling, though. She knew that choosing to become a nurse would mean going against everything her family and society expected of her. It would mean giving up the comfortable life that had been planned for her, a life of luxury and ease. But Florence couldn't ignore the voice inside her. It was persistent, never letting her forget that she had a higher purpose.

One evening, when Florence was about sixteen years old, she had an experience that would change her life forever. She was walking alone in the garden of her family's estate, thinking about the future and the choices she would have to make. As she walked, she felt a deep sense of peace and clarity come over her. In that moment, she felt as if she could hear God speaking to her, telling her that she was meant to serve others through nursing. It was a powerful, almost overwhelming experience, and it left no doubt in Florence's mind about what she had to do. This was the moment when Florence knew, with absolute certainty, that she had been called to be a nurse.

This wasn't something Florence could easily share with her family. She knew that her parents had different plans for her and that they wouldn't understand why she felt so strongly about nursing. But Florence was determined to follow the path that had been laid out for her, no matter how difficult it might be. She began to prepare herself for the challenges ahead, studying everything she could about health, medicine, and nursing. She read books, observed medical practices, and learned from anyone who could teach her something useful. Florence was determined to be the best nurse she could be, even if she had to do it all on her own.

Florence's family, especially her mother, was concerned about the path she was choosing. They couldn't understand why she would want to throw away the advantages of her birth and position to do something so beneath her station. Her mother, Frances, was particularly upset. She had always imagined a bright future for Florence, filled with social events, marriage, and children. Nursing, in her eyes, was a waste of Florence's talents and potential.

But Florence's mind was made up. She respected her parents and loved them dearly, but she couldn't ignore the calling she felt. She knew that following this path would not be easy, and that it would require sacrifices. She also knew that she might never gain her family's approval. But none of that mattered as much as staying true to herself and to the voice she believed was guiding her.

There were many times when Florence doubted herself, when the pressure to conform to society's expectations seemed almost too much to bear. But every time she felt like giving up, she would remember that moment in the garden, when she had felt so certain of her purpose. That memory gave her strength and kept her moving forward, even when the road ahead seemed impossible.

As Florence continued to pursue her dream of becoming a nurse, she faced resistance not just from her family, but from society as a whole. People didn't understand why a wealthy, educated woman would want to lower herself to do such work. They questioned her sanity, her judgment, and even her character. But Florence wasn't deterred. She knew that her calling was real, and she wasn't going to let anyone stand in her way.

Florence's determination to follow her calling led her to seek out opportunities to learn and practice nursing, even when it meant going against her family's wishes. She traveled to different countries to study how hospitals were run, and she volunteered in places where she could gain practical experience. Each step she took brought her closer to fulfilling the destiny she had felt since she was a child.

Florence's story is a powerful reminder that sometimes, the path we are meant to follow isn't the one that others expect us to take. It can be difficult to go against the grain, to stand up for what we believe in, especially when it means disappointing the people we care about. But Florence's life shows us that when we listen to the voice inside us, the one that tells us who we really are and what we are meant to do, we can find the courage to follow our own path.

overcoming obstacles

In the 1800s, society had very strict ideas about what women should and shouldn't do. For a girl like Florence, born into a wealthy family, the expectations were even more rigid. Women of her class were expected to live quiet, comfortable lives. They were supposed to focus on finding a suitable husband, running a household, and raising children. Pursuing a career, especially one like nursing, was considered improper and unnecessary.

Nursing, in particular, had a reputation that made it seem unsuitable for a woman of Florence's status. It was seen as dirty, grueling work that was done by women who had no other options in life. Nurses were often untrained and worked in poor conditions, caring for patients in filthy hospitals where disease spread easily. It was not a job that society admired or respected, and certainly not a profession that a young woman from a wealthy family would be encouraged to pursue.

But Florence saw things differently. She saw

nursing as a noble calling, a way to make a real difference in the world. She believed that with proper training and care, nurses could save lives and improve the health and well-being of countless people. However, convincing others of this, especially her family, was another matter entirely.

Florence's parents, William and Frances Nightingale, had their own ideas about what was best for their daughter. They loved Florence dearly and wanted her to have a good life—a life that, in their minds, involved marrying well and taking her place in society. They couldn't understand why she would want to throw all of that away to do something as difficult and unglamorous as nursing.

Florence's mother, Frances, was particularly opposed to the idea. She had always hoped that Florence would follow the traditional path expected of a woman of her standing. Frances worried that nursing would ruin Florence's chances of finding a suitable husband and living the kind of life that was considered appropriate for someone of her social class. To Frances, the idea of her daughter working in hospitals, surrounded by sickness and death, was unthinkable.

Florence's father, William, was more supportive of her education and intellectual pursuits, but even he had reservations about her becoming a nurse.

He understood her desire to help others, but he also recognized the obstacles she would face in a society that didn't value women in the workforce, especially in a role like nursing. He knew that Florence would have to battle not just societal expectations, but also the prejudice and judgment of those around her.

Despite their concerns, Florence was determined. She felt that her calling to be a nurse was too strong to ignore, and she was willing to face whatever challenges came her way. But this determination didn't make things any easier. The more Florence insisted on pursuing nursing, the more tension grew within her family.

There were arguments and disagreements, with Florence trying to explain why nursing was so important to her and her parents trying to convince her to choose a different path. These weren't easy conversations. Florence loved her family and respected their opinions, but she also knew that she couldn't live a life that wasn't true to who she was. This inner conflict weighed heavily on her, but it also strengthened her resolve.

One of the biggest challenges Florence faced was the isolation that came with her decision. By choosing a path that went against societal norms, Florence found herself feeling alone at times. Most of her friends and peers didn't understand her passion for nursing. They were focused on their own lives, attending social events, and planning their futures in ways that aligned with society's expectations. Florence, on the other hand, was consumed by her desire to help others, to make a difference in the world, even if it meant stepping away from the life she had always known.

But Florence didn't let this isolation deter her. Instead, she sought out opportunities to learn more about nursing and healthcare. She read medical books, studied the workings of hospitals, and sought advice from doctors and other healthcare professionals. She even visited hospitals and observed the conditions there, determined to understand what needed to be done to improve them.

Florence's persistence eventually led her to Kaiserswerth, a small town in Germany where there was a Protestant community that ran a hospital and school for training nurses. This was one of the few places in Europe where women could receive formal training in nursing. Florence knew that this was an opportunity she couldn't pass up, even though it meant leaving her family and facing even more disapproval from those around her.

At Kaiserswerth, Florence found herself surrounded by others who shared her passion for nursing and healthcare. She finally had the chance to learn the skills she would need to fulfill her calling. But even here, the challenges continued. The training was rigorous, the work was demanding, and the conditions were far from comfortable. Florence had to work long hours, often in difficult and emotionally draining situations. But she thrived in this environment, learning quickly and proving herself to be an exceptionally skilled and compassionate nurse.

When Florence returned to England after her training, she was more determined than ever to pursue her career in nursing. But the obstacles she faced weren't just limited to her family's disapproval. Society at large still held deeply ingrained prejudices against women in the workforce, especially in roles like nursing. Florence knew that if she was going to make a difference, she would have to challenge these prejudices head-on.

Florence began to write about her experiences and her ideas for reforming hospitals and nursing practices. She argued that nursing was not only a respectable profession but an essential one. She emphasized the importance of proper training, cleanliness, and organization in hospitals—ideas that were revolutionary at the time. Her writings began to attract attention, and slowly, people started to take her seriously.

But this newfound attention also brought new challenges. Florence found herself the subject of gossip and criticism from those who didn't agree with her ideas. She was accused of being too radical, of trying to push women into roles that weren't meant for them. But Florence didn't let these criticisms stop her. She knew that what she was doing was important, and she wasn't going to let anyone stand in her way.

education and training

Florence's fascination with medicine began at a young age. As a child, she was curious about how the human body worked and why people became ill. While other girls her age were content with playing games and practicing their social graces, Florence was more interested in reading books about anatomy and science. She would spend hours in her father's library, absorbed in medical texts that were far beyond what most children, or even adults, were reading. This was not just a hobby for her—it was a passion that grew stronger with each passing year.

Despite the limitations placed on women's education at the time, Florence's parents recognized her intelligence and provided her with access to the best tutors. She studied subjects like mathematics, philosophy, and languages, all of which helped her develop the analytical skills she would later use in her nursing career. However, formal education in medicine was not something that was typically offered to women, especially those from wealthy families. Florence had to seek out knowledge on her own, often teaching herself through reading and observation.

Florence's first real experience with nursing came when she was a teenager. During a visit to a village near her family's estate, she encountered a poor family living in dreadful conditions. The mother was gravely ill, and the children were dirty and malnourished. Florence immediately took charge, cleaning the house, caring for the children, and nursing the mother back to health. This experience had a profound impact on her. It reinforced her belief that nursing was her calling and showed her that she had a natural talent for it.

But Florence knew that natural talent alone wasn't enough. She needed proper training to become the kind of nurse who could truly make a difference. This realization drove her to seek out any opportunity to learn about medicine and healthcare, even if it meant going against her family's wishes and society's expectations.

One of the most significant steps in Florence's education came when she convinced her parents to allow her to visit hospitals. At the time, hospitals were not places where respectable women went, especially not for the purpose of learning. But Florence was determined. She visited hospitals in London, observing the conditions, talking to the staff, and taking notes on what she saw. These visits were eye-opening for Florence. She saw first-hand how poorly many hospitals were run, with overcrowded wards, dirty facilities, and a lack of proper medical care. These observations fueled her desire to improve hospital conditions and provide better care for patients.

Florence's hunger for knowledge led her to Kaiserswerth, a small town in Germany where there was a Protestant community that ran a hospital and a school for training nurses. This was one of the few places in Europe where women could receive formal training in nursing. Florence knew that this was the opportunity she had been waiting for. Although her family was reluctant to let her go, they eventually agreed, recognizing that this was something Florence was deeply committed to.

At Kaiserswerth, Florence finally received the hands-on training she had been seeking. The program was rigorous, with long hours spent caring for patients, learning about hygiene, and studying medical techniques. The conditions were far from luxurious; the hospital was a modest facility, and the work was physically and emotionally demanding. But Florence thrived in this environment. She absorbed everything she could, learning not just about nursing, but also about hospital administration and public health. She was particularly interested in how to organize hospitals in a way that would prevent the spread of disease and improve patient outcomes.

One of the most valuable lessons Florence learned at Kaiserswerth was the importance of cleanliness in hospitals. At the time, the connection between hygiene and health was not well understood. Many hospitals were breeding grounds for infections, and patients often left the hospital sicker than when they arrived. Florence learned about the importance of sterilizing equipment, washing hands, and keeping the hospital environment clean. These lessons would later become central to her work in reforming hospitals and improving patient care.

Florence's time at Kaiserswerth was transformative. She returned to England with a new sense of purpose and a wealth of knowledge that would set the foundation for her future work. But her education didn't stop there. Florence continued to seek out learning opportunities wherever she could find them. She read medical journals, corresponded with doctors, and studied the latest developments in healthcare. She was particularly interested in statistics and how they could be used to improve public health. Florence became one of the first people to use statistical analysis to track the spread of disease and identify the most effective treatments.

Florence's commitment to her education and training was driven by her belief that knowledge was the key to making a real difference in the world. She didn't just want to be a nurse—she wanted to be the best nurse she could be, one who was equipped with the skills and knowledge needed to save lives and improve the healthcare system. This dedication to learning set her apart from others and helped her overcome the many obstacles she faced on her journey.

3 /

the crimean war

crimean war and why it was significant

THE CRIMEAN WAR was one of those conflicts that changed the course of history, but it wasn't just about battles and territories. It was a war that highlighted the importance of healthcare and the need for reform, something that Florence Nightingale would soon become deeply involved in. To understand why this war was significant, it's important to take a closer look at what led to it and why it mattered to so many countries.

The Crimean War began in 1853 and lasted until 1856, involving several of the world's major powers at the time. The main countries involved were Russia, the Ottoman Empire (which is present-day

Turkey), France, and Britain. But what could cause such powerful nations to go to war with each other? The answer lies in a complex mix of politics, religion, and the struggle for power.

At the heart of the conflict was the declining Ottoman Empire, which had once been a dominant force in the world but was now weakening. As the Ottoman Empire lost its grip on its territories, other powerful nations saw an opportunity to expand their influence. Russia, in particular, was interested in gaining more control over the regions around the Black Sea, an area that was crucial for trade and military strategy. The Russian Empire, under Tsar Nicholas I, wanted access to warm-water ports, which would allow Russian ships to operate year-round. However, gaining control of these ports meant encroaching on the territory of the Ottoman Empire.

The conflict began to escalate over religious issues. The Russian Empire, which was predominantly Orthodox Christian, claimed to have the right to protect Orthodox Christians living within the Ottoman Empire. This claim was partly a pretext for expanding Russian influence in the region, but it also sparked tensions with the Ottoman rulers, who were Muslim. France, on the other hand, had a long-standing role as the protector of Catholics in the Ottoman Empire, and they were not willing to let Russia gain more influence.

The situation quickly spiraled out of control. The Ottoman Empire, feeling threatened by Russia's demands, declared war on Russia in October 1853. Britain and France, concerned about Russia's growing power and eager to maintain the balance of power in Europe, soon joined the Ottomans in the fight against Russia. Austria and Prussia, two other major powers of the time, remained neutral but were closely watching the situation.

For the countries involved, the Crimean War was about more than just territory—it was about maintaining influence and power in Europe. If Russia succeeded in its goals, it could upset the balance of power that had kept Europe relatively stable for decades. Britain, in particular, was concerned about Russia's ambitions. They didn't want Russia to gain control of the eastern Mediterranean, which could threaten Britain's trade routes to India and the rest of its empire.

The war was named after the Crimean Peninsula, a region on the northern coast of the Black Sea, where much of the fighting took place. The most famous battle of the war was the Siege of

Sevastopol, a major port city on the peninsula. The siege lasted for almost a year and was one of the longest and bloodiest conflicts of the war. The conditions during the siege were horrific, with soldiers on both sides suffering from disease, cold, and starvation, in addition to the dangers of battle.

For the soldiers who fought in the Crimean War, the experience was brutal. The war was one of the first to be heavily covered by journalists, and reports of the terrible conditions faced by soldiers shocked the public back home. The British and French armies, in particular, were ill-prepared for the harsh conditions of the Crimean winter. Many soldiers died not from battle wounds but from diseases like cholera, dysentery, and typhus, which spread rapidly in the overcrowded and unsanitary camps.

It was these reports of suffering that caught the attention of Florence Nightingale, who was already deeply concerned about the state of healthcare in Britain and its military. When she read about the appalling conditions in the military hospitals, she knew that this was where she needed to be. Florence saw the war as an opportunity to put her skills and knowledge to the test, and to make a real difference in the lives of those who were suffering.

The Crimean War was also significant for the

way it changed public perceptions of war and healthcare. For the first time, people back home were getting a glimpse of the realities of war, not just through official reports, but through the stories and letters of the soldiers themselves. The war was one of the first to be covered by war correspondents, and their reports brought the horrors of the battlefield into the living rooms of ordinary people. This new level of awareness led to a growing demand for better care for soldiers and for reforms in the way military hospitals were run.

Florence Nightingale's decision to go to the Crimea was not just about nursing—it was about responding to a crisis that was unfolding on a global stage. She understood that the war presented a unique opportunity to make lasting changes in the way healthcare was delivered, both in the military and in society at large. Her work during the Crimean War would not only save countless lives but also set new standards for nursing and hospital care that would influence the future of medicine.

florence goes to war

Florence had spent years preparing herself for this moment, studying medicine, visiting hospitals, and learning everything she could about nursing. But now it was time to put that knowledge into action. She was determined to go to the Crimea and make a difference, but she knew that she couldn't do it alone. Florence needed a team of skilled and dedicated nurses to help her tackle the enormous task that lay ahead.

At that time, the idea of women going to war to nurse soldiers was almost unheard of. Nursing was not considered a respectable profession for women, especially not in a war zone. But Florence wasn't one to be deterred by societal expectations. She believed that if women were properly trained, they could provide the care that the soldiers so desperately needed. With this belief in mind, she set out to recruit a team of nurses who were willing to leave behind their comfortable lives and face the dangers of war.

Florence's first step was to write to Sidney Herbert, the Secretary of War. Herbert was a close friend and supporter of Florence's work, and he had been instrumental in encouraging her to take on this mission. Florence explained the dire situation in the military hospitals and made it clear that immediate action was needed. She offered to lead a team of nurses to the Crimea, where they could provide the care that was so desperately lacking.

Herbert agreed, recognizing that Florence was uniquely qualified for the task.

With Herbert's backing, Florence began the difficult process of selecting her team. She knew that this wasn't just about finding women who were willing to help; they had to be strong, resilient, and able to handle the harsh conditions they would face. Florence placed an advertisement in newspapers, calling for volunteers who were experienced in nursing or who had the qualities needed to be trained quickly. The response was overwhelming. Women from all walks of life applied, eager to join Florence on her mission. Some were experienced nurses, while others were simply motivated by a desire to help.

Florence was meticulous in her selection process. She interviewed each applicant personally, looking for qualities like compassion, determination, and the ability to work under pressure. She needed women who were not only skilled but also had the emotional strength to deal with the horrors they would witness. In the end, she selected 38 women—24 were experienced nurses, and the remaining 14 were nuns who had experience in caring for the sick.

Once the team was assembled, Florence wasted no time in preparing them for the journey ahead.

They gathered supplies, including medical equipment, clothing, and food, knowing that they couldn't rely on the military to provide everything they needed. Florence also took the time to train her team, teaching them about hygiene, wound care, and how to prevent the spread of disease. She knew that their success would depend on their ability to work together as a cohesive unit, and she made sure that everyone understood their role.

On October 21, 1854, Florence and her team set sail for the Crimea. The journey was long and perilous, taking them across the treacherous waters of the Mediterranean Sea. As they traveled, Florence used the time to continue training her nurses and to plan for the challenges they would face once they arrived. She knew that the conditions would be far worse than anything they had encountered in England, but she was determined to be ready.

When they finally arrived in Constantinople (modern-day Istanbul), they were greeted with a scene of utter chaos. The military hospital at Scutari, where they were to work, was in a state of complete disarray. The building was overcrowded with wounded soldiers, many of whom were lying on the floor without even a blanket to cover them. The smell of rotting flesh and human waste filled the air, and rats scurried through the corridors. It was a scene that would have broken the spirit of many, but not Florence. She knew that this was exactly why she had come, and she was determined to make a difference.

Florence and her team immediately set to work. They began by cleaning the hospital from top to bottom, scrubbing the floors, washing the bedding, and clearing away the filth that had accumulated over months of neglect. They organized the wards, ensuring that each patient had a clean bed and that the most seriously wounded were given priority. Florence introduced strict rules for hygiene, insisting that everyone wash their hands regularly and that all medical instruments be sterilized. These measures, though basic by today's standards, were revolutionary at the time and had an immediate impact on the health and well-being of the soldiers.

But Florence's work didn't stop at improving the physical conditions of the hospital. She understood that the soldiers needed more than just medical care—they needed emotional support as well. Many of the men were far from home, scared, and in pain. Florence made it a point to spend time with each patient, talking to them, listening to their stories, and offering words of comfort. She became a source of strength and hope for the soldiers, who began to see her as a guardian angel. It was during this time that she earned the nickname "The Lady with the Lamp," because of her habit of making nightly rounds to check on the men, often carrying a small lamp to light her way.

Florence's leadership and determination inspired her team to keep going, even when the work seemed overwhelming. There were times when they were exhausted, working long hours in difficult conditions, but Florence's example kept them focused on their mission. She had a clear vision of what needed to be done, and she wasn't afraid to make difficult decisions or to stand up to military authorities when necessary.

One of the biggest challenges Florence faced was dealing with the military bureaucracy. The army was not used to having women in positions of authority, and there were many who resented Florence's presence. Some officers tried to undermine her efforts, questioning her methods and her authority. But Florence was not easily intimidated. She fought for the supplies and support her team needed, often going directly to high-ranking officials to make her case. Her persistence paid off, and over time, she gained the respect and cooperation of many in the military.

transforming hospitals

When Florence Nightingale arrived at the military hospitals in the Crimea, she was met with a sight that would have horrified even the most seasoned nurse. The hospitals, which were supposed to be places of healing, were more like death traps. The conditions were beyond terrible, with overcrowded wards, filthy environments, and a lack of basic medical supplies. Soldiers who had survived the horrors of the battlefield were now facing a new battle—one against disease, infection, and neglect.

The hospital at Scutari, where Florence and her team of nurses were stationed, was perhaps the worst of all. The building itself was never designed to be a hospital; it was an old, run-down barracks that had been hastily converted into a medical facility when the war broke out. The wards were overcrowded with injured soldiers, many of whom were lying on the floor because there weren't enough beds. The air was thick with the stench of sweat, blood, and unwashed bodies. The walls were grimy, the floors were covered in filth, and rats and insects were everywhere. To make matters worse, there was almost no ventilation, which meant that the air inside the hospital was stagnant and filled with disease-causing germs.

Florence knew that if she didn't act quickly, more soldiers would die—not from their injuries, but from the appalling conditions in the hospital. She wasted no time in assessing the situation and coming up with a plan. Her first priority was to improve the cleanliness and hygiene of the hospital, which she knew was essential to preventing the spread of disease.

One of the first changes Florence implemented was a strict regime of cleaning and sanitation. She organized her team of nurses and the orderlies to scrub the floors, walls, and ceilings of the hospital from top to bottom. Every inch of the building was cleaned, and the filthy bedding was removed and replaced with clean linens. Florence also insisted that the soldiers themselves be cleaned and their wounds properly dressed. This was a daunting task, as many of the soldiers were too weak to move, but Florence and her team worked tirelessly to ensure that every patient received the care they needed.

Florence also tackled the problem of overcrowding. She reorganized the wards, moving the most seriously injured soldiers to quieter areas where they could rest and recover. She made sure that each patient had enough space around their bed to allow for proper air circulation, which was crucial in preventing the spread of infection. She even went so far as to remove some of the patients from the hospital altogether, setting up makeshift wards in nearby buildings to alleviate the overcrowding.

But Florence's changes didn't stop at cleaning and reorganizing. She recognized that the soldiers needed more than just a clean environment—they needed proper nutrition and medical care as well. The food that was being provided to the soldiers was inadequate and often inedible. The kitchens were dirty, and the food was poorly prepared, leading to malnutrition and further weakening the already vulnerable patients.

Florence took charge of the kitchen, ensuring that the soldiers received nutritious meals that would help them regain their strength. She introduced simple but healthy foods, such as soups made from fresh vegetables and meat, which were easier for the soldiers to digest and provided them with the necessary nutrients to heal. She also made sure that the food was prepared in a clean environment and that the cooks and kitchen staff followed proper hygiene practices.

In addition to improving the food, Florence made sure that the soldiers had access to clean water. The hospital's water supply was contaminated, which was contributing to the spread of diseases like cholera and dysentery. Florence arranged for fresh water to be brought in, and she oversaw the installation of new plumbing systems that provided clean water for drinking, cooking, and washing.

One of the most important changes Florence made was in the area of medical care. When she first arrived, the hospital was severely under-staffed, and the few doctors who were there were overwhelmed by the sheer number of patients. There were also very few medical supplies, and what little they had was often dirty or outdated. Florence worked tirelessly to improve the situation. She wrote letters to government officials and chari-table organizations back in England, requesting more doctors, nurses, and medical supplies. She also kept detailed records of the hospital's needs and the progress being made, which helped her make a strong case for the improvements she was seeking.

Florence's efforts began to pay off. As the hospital became cleaner and more organized, the death rate among the soldiers started to decline. Diseases that had once been rampant began to subside, and the soldiers who had been on the brink of death were now starting to recover. The changes Florence implemented were simple but effective, and they demonstrated the power of basic hygiene and proper care in saving lives.

But Florence's work didn't stop with the physical improvements to the hospital. She also focused on the mental and emotional well-being of the soldiers. She understood that many of the men were suffering not just from physical wounds, but from the trauma of war. They were far from home, scared, and uncertain about their future. Florence made it a point to spend time with each soldier, talking to them, offering words of comfort, and listening to their concerns. She encouraged her nurses to do the same, creating an environment of care and compassion that was as important to the soldiers' recovery as the medical treatment they received.

Florence's commitment to her work and her belief in the importance of proper care inspired everyone around her. Her nurses, who had been overwhelmed by the conditions they encountered when they first arrived, now found themselves motivated by Florence's example. They worked long hours, often going without sleep, to ensure that every patient received the best care possible. Even the doctors and military officials, who had initially been skeptical of Florence's methods, began to see the value of her approach.

4 /

the lady with the lamp

florence's night rounds

FLORENCE WAS tireless in her dedication to the men under her care. By day, she managed the hospital with a firm yet compassionate hand, ensuring that every aspect of the soldiers' treatment was handled with care. But it was at night, when the rest of the hospital staff was either resting or tending to other duties, that Florence would take up her lamp and make her rounds. She knew that the night brought with it a different kind of suffering, one that often went unseen and unaddressed, and she wasn't willing to let her soldiers endure it alone.

.   .   .

The image of Florence Nightingale, her figure softly illuminated by the warm glow of a small oil lamp, moving silently through the wards, became one of the most enduring symbols of her work. This nightly ritual was more than just a check on the patients' physical well-being; it was a way of offering comfort and reassurance to the men who were battling not just their injuries, but the emotional toll of war.

Florence's night rounds were conducted with the same meticulous attention to detail that she applied to everything else. She would start at one end of the hospital and work her way through each ward, stopping at every bed to check on the soldiers. She looked for signs of infection, monitored their wounds, and made sure they were comfortable. If a bandage needed changing, she would do it herself. If a soldier was feverish, she would cool his forehead with a damp cloth. If a patient was thirsty, she would bring him water. Nothing was too small for Florence to notice, and nothing was too insignificant for her to address.

•　•　•

But it wasn't just the physical care that mattered. Florence understood that the soldiers were scared, homesick, and often overwhelmed by the horrors they had witnessed on the battlefield. The sight of her approaching lamp was a beacon of hope, a sign that someone cared enough to watch over them, even in the darkest hours. Many of the soldiers were too weak to speak, but the gratitude in their eyes as she approached spoke volumes. Florence's presence was a comfort, a reminder that they were not forgotten, that someone was there to care for them when they needed it most.

The nickname "The Lady with the Lamp" wasn't something Florence sought out or even knew about at first. It was given to her by the soldiers, who saw her as a guardian angel moving through the night, bringing light and care to the wounded. The soldiers would later write about her in letters to their families, describing how she would appear at their bedside when they were at their lowest, offering words of encouragement or simply sitting with them for a few moments in silence. These small acts of kindness made a tremendous impact on the men, many of whom felt abandoned by their country and forgotten by the world.

. . .

Florence's night rounds were not just about attending to the soldiers' needs. They were also about gathering information. As she moved through the wards, she would make mental notes of anything that seemed off—a cough that sounded worse than before, a wound that wasn't healing as it should, a patient who seemed more despondent than usual. The next day, she would follow up on these observations, making sure that the necessary treatments were administered and that the doctors were aware of any changes in the patients' conditions. This level of care was unprecedented, and it was one of the reasons why the death rate in the hospital began to drop under Florence's watch.

The soldiers weren't the only ones who noticed Florence's dedication. The other nurses and even the doctors began to look to her as a leader and an example of what true nursing should be. Her tireless work ethic, her attention to detail, and her deep compassion for the patients inspired those around her to work harder and to care more deeply. Florence's night rounds became a sort of ritual, something that everyone in the hospital came to expect and rely on.

As word of her nightly visits spread, Florence became a symbol of hope not just in the Crimea, but back in England as well. Reports of her work were sent home by journalists, and soon the entire nation knew about "The Lady with the Lamp." She became a hero, not because of any grand gestures, but because of the simple, consistent acts of care and kindness that she showed to those in need.

caring for the soldiers

Florence Nightingale's work in the Crimean War wasn't just about improving hospital conditions or introducing better medical practices. It was about the personal, heartfelt care she provided to the soldiers who were suffering, both physically and emotionally. Her compassion and dedication went far beyond the call of duty, and it's in the stories of how she cared for the wounded soldiers that we see the true impact of her work.

. . .

One story that illustrates Florence's deep compassion involves a young soldier named William. William had been severely wounded in battle, and by the time he arrived at the hospital in Scutari, his condition was critical. He had lost a lot of blood and was suffering from a terrible infection. The doctors had done what they could, but they didn't hold out much hope for his recovery. William was in tremendous pain, and he was terrified—scared not just of dying, but of dying alone, far from his family and friends.

Florence noticed William's distress during one of her night rounds. She saw the fear in his eyes and the way he clenched his fists in pain. Instead of just moving on to the next patient, she sat down beside him and took his hand. She spoke to him softly, asking about his family, where he was from, and what he had done before the war. William was too weak to say much, but he managed to tell Florence about his mother and how he missed home. Florence listened with deep empathy, understanding that what William needed most in that moment was not more medicine, but the comfort of knowing someone cared.

• • •

Florence stayed with William for hours that night, holding his hand and reassuring him that he wasn't alone. She made sure that he was as comfortable as possible, adjusting his pillows, cooling his forehead with a damp cloth, and speaking to him in a soothing voice. Over the next few days, she continued to visit him regularly, offering comfort and care. William's condition eventually stabilized, and he began to recover. He later told his fellow soldiers that it was Florence's kindness and the simple act of holding his hand that had given him the strength to keep fighting. For William, Florence wasn't just a nurse—she was a lifeline, a beacon of hope in his darkest hour.

Another story that highlights Florence's dedication involves a group of soldiers who had been severely wounded in a battle near Balaclava. These men were brought to the hospital at Scutari in a terrible state, many of them suffering from multiple injuries, infections, and frostbite. The conditions in which they had been fighting were brutal, and the journey to the hospital had only worsened their condition. When they arrived, the hospital was already overcrowded, and there was a shortage of beds, medical supplies, and even food.

. . .

Florence immediately recognized the gravity of the situation. She knew that these men needed more than just basic care—they needed intensive, around-the-clock attention if they were to have any chance of survival. She organized her team of nurses, assigning them to specific patients and ensuring that each man received the care he needed. But Florence didn't just direct others; she led by example.

One of the soldiers in this group was a man named Thomas. He had been hit by shrapnel and had also suffered severe frostbite on his hands and feet. His wounds were infected, and he was in excruciating pain. The doctors were concerned that they might have to amputate his limbs, and Thomas was terrified at the thought of losing his hands and feet. Florence took a special interest in Thomas's case, determined to save his limbs if at all possible.

She worked tirelessly to clean and dress his wounds, carefully applying ointments and bandages to prevent further infection. She also made sure that Thomas was kept warm, wrapping him in blankets and massaging his hands and feet to improve circulation. Florence spent hours by his bedside, talking to him, encouraging him, and distracting him from the pain. Her dedication paid off. Over time, Thomas's condition improved, and the doctors were able to save his limbs. He later credited Florence with saving not just his life, but his ability to walk and work again.

Florence's impact wasn't limited to the physical care she provided. She understood that the mental and emotional well-being of the soldiers was just as important as their physical health. Many of the men were struggling with the trauma of war—the memories of battles, the loss of comrades, and the fear of what lay ahead. Florence made it a point to address these emotional wounds, offering a kind word, a listening ear, or just a presence that reassured the soldiers they were not alone.

One of the soldiers, James, had been a strong and confident man before the war, but after months of fighting, he was a shadow of his former self. The horrors he had witnessed on the battlefield had left him withdrawn and depressed. He had lost the will to fight, and even though his physical wounds were healing, he was sinking deeper into despair.

Florence noticed the change in James and decided to intervene. She began visiting him regularly, not to check his wounds, but simply to talk. She encouraged him to share his feelings, to talk about what he had seen and experienced. Florence didn't judge or offer empty platitudes; she simply listened, offering understanding and support. Over time, James began to open up, and the weight of his trauma started to lift. Florence's compassion helped him find the strength to keep going, and he eventually made a full recovery, both physically and mentally.

Florence's compassion extended beyond the individual soldiers. She cared deeply about the welfare of all the men under her care, and she fought tirelessly to improve their living conditions. She advocated for better food, cleaner water, and more comfortable bedding. She made sure that the soldiers had access to letters from home, recognizing the importance of maintaining a connection to their families. Florence even took the time to write letters on behalf of soldiers who were too weak to do so themselves, ensuring that their loved ones knew they were still alive and receiving care.

the power of compassion

One of the most profound lessons from Florence's life is that compassion can change the world, one person at a time. In the crowded, dirty hospitals of Scutari, where soldiers lay in pain and fear, Florence's compassion became a beacon of hope. She didn't see the soldiers as just patients or cases to be managed; she saw them as individuals with their own stories, families, and dreams. This empathy drove her to go beyond the basic duties of nursing. She treated each soldier with dignity and respect, recognizing their humanity in the most difficult circumstances.

Empathy, the ability to understand and share the feelings of another, was something Florence practiced every day. She knew that being a good nurse wasn't just about applying bandages or giving medicine; it was about connecting with the person you were caring for. Florence would sit by the bedsides of the soldiers, listening to their stories, their fears, and their hopes. She didn't just offer medical care; she offered a human connection. This connection helped the soldiers feel less alone, less abandoned in a foreign land far from home.

One powerful example of Florence's empathy was how she handled the emotional wounds of the soldiers, wounds that were often invisible but just as painful as physical injuries. War is a traumatic experience, and many of the soldiers were haunted by what they had seen and done. Florence understood that healing the body was only part of the battle; healing the mind and spirit was just as important. By taking the time to talk with the soldiers, to listen without judgment, Florence helped them begin to process their trauma. She provided a safe space where they could express their fears and grief, something that was essential for their overall recovery.

Florence's compassion also extended to her fellow nurses. Leading a team of women in such a challenging environment required not just authority, but understanding. Florence was aware of the emotional toll that caring for the wounded could take on her nurses. She made sure to support them, to listen to their concerns, and to provide them with the encouragement they needed to continue their difficult work. Her kindness created a sense of camaraderie among the nurses, helping them to form a strong, supportive team that could handle the immense challenges they faced.

One of the most enduring lessons from Florence's life is that small acts of kindness can have a ripple effect, spreading outwards and touching more lives than we might ever realize. Florence's nightly rounds, where she checked on each soldier personally, were one such act. To the soldiers, seeing Florence with her lamp, moving quietly through the darkened wards, was a reminder that someone cared. These moments of kindness gave the soldiers strength and comfort during their darkest hours. And as word of her compassionate care spread, Florence became a symbol of hope not just for the men in the hospital, but for people around the world.

. . .

The power of compassion lies in its ability to connect people. Florence understood that everyone, no matter their rank or background, deserved to be treated with kindness and respect. She didn't see herself as superior to the soldiers or even to the orderlies and other hospital staff. Instead, she saw herself as part of a larger effort to care for those in need. This humility and sense of shared purpose were at the core of her approach to nursing, and they inspired others to follow her example.

Florence's legacy teaches us that compassion isn't just a personal virtue; it's a social one. The changes she made in the hospitals—improving hygiene, organizing care, and advocating for better conditions—were all driven by her belief that society has a responsibility to care for its most vulnerable members. Florence's work helped to lay the foundation for modern nursing and public health, and it showed that compassionate care isn't just about treating illness; it's about promoting the well-being of the whole person and the community.

a legacy of change

after the war

WHEN THE CRIMEAN War finally ended, Florence Nightingale returned to England as a hero. The newspapers had told stories of "The Lady with the Lamp," and her work had made her famous. But despite all the praise and recognition, Florence wasn't interested in resting on her laurels. The war might have been over, but Florence knew that her work was just beginning. She had seen firsthand the terrible conditions in the hospitals, and she was determined to make sure that no one ever had to suffer like that again.

Back in England, Florence faced a new challenge: how to take everything she had learned during the war and use it to improve healthcare for everyone. She was deeply committed to the idea that the lessons from the war shouldn't just stay in the past—they needed to be applied to hospitals and medical practices across the country and even beyond.

Florence's first step was to gather data. She was a firm believer in the power of facts and statistics, and she knew that to convince others of the need for change, she would need hard evidence. She began by meticulously documenting everything she had observed during the war. She collected information on death rates, the causes of illness, and the effectiveness of different treatments. This wasn't just about numbers for Florence; it was about showing that the right care could save lives and that the wrong conditions could cost them.

One of Florence's major achievements after the war was her work on the Royal Commission on the Health of the Army. This commission was set up to investigate the conditions in military hospitals and to recommend improvements. Florence played a key role in the commission's work, using her data to argue for better hygiene, proper nutrition, and more organized medical care. She didn't just present problems—she offered solutions, based on her experiences in the Crimea.

But Florence's vision went beyond just

improving military hospitals. She wanted to change the way nursing was practiced everywhere. During the war, she had seen how proper nursing care could make a real difference, and she believed that the key to better healthcare was better training for nurses. At that time, nursing wasn't seen as a respectable profession, and there was little formal training available. Florence wanted to change that.

She began by establishing the Nightingale Training School for Nurses at St. Thomas' Hospital in London. This school was revolutionary because it was one of the first to offer formal education and training specifically for nurses. Florence's curriculum emphasized not just medical knowledge, but also the importance of cleanliness, compassion, and patient care. She believed that nurses needed to be both skilled and caring, and her school was designed to produce exactly that kind of nurse.

The Nightingale Training School quickly gained a reputation for excellence, and its graduates were in high demand. These nurses didn't just work in hospitals—they went on to spread Florence's ideas and practices wherever they went. Many of them became leaders in their own right, establishing nursing schools and hospitals in other parts of the world. In this way, Florence's influence extended far beyond the walls of her own school.

Florence also used her fame and influence to advocate for broader public health reforms. She wrote extensively on topics like sanitation, hospital design, and the importance of clean water. Her book, Notes on Nursing: What It Is and What It Is Not, became a best-seller and was widely read by both medical professionals and ordinary people. In it, Florence laid out the basic principles of good nursing care, emphasizing the need for cleanliness, fresh air, and proper diet. The book was practical and accessible, making it an essential guide for anyone involved in healthcare.

But Florence's work didn't stop there. She was deeply concerned about the health of the poor and vulnerable, and she worked tirelessly to improve conditions in hospitals and workhouses (places where the poor could live and work). She believed that everyone, regardless of their social status, deserved to be cared for when they were sick. To Florence, nursing wasn't just a job—it was a calling, and it was about serving those in need.

One of the ways Florence tried to make health-care more accessible was by working with architects to design better hospitals. She believed that the environment in which patients were treated had a huge impact on their recovery. Hospitals, she argued, should be clean, well-ventilated, and designed with the needs of patients in mind. She promoted the idea of "pavilion" style hospitals, with separate wings for different types of patients, which allowed for better ventilation and more effective infection control. Her ideas were ahead of their time, but they eventually became standard practice in hospital design.

revolutionizing healthcare

When Florence began her work, nursing was not seen as a respected profession. In fact, it was often considered a job for those who had few other options. Nurses were typically untrained, and hospitals were grim, unsanitary places where people went as a last resort. Florence set out to change that perception. She believed that nursing was a vital and honorable profession, and she knew that proper training was essential to elevate it to the level of respect it deserved.

One of Florence's most significant contributions to modern nursing was her emphasis on education. She understood that in order to provide the best care, nurses needed more than just a kind heart— they needed knowledge and skills. This was a radical idea at the time, but Florence was determined to prove its value. She designed a comprehensive curriculum for her nursing school that included not only the practical skills of nursing, such as how to dress wounds and administer medicine, but also subjects like anatomy, physiology, and public health. Florence believed that nurses should be well-rounded professionals, equipped with a deep understanding of the human body and the factors that affect health.

The success of the Nightingale Training School for Nurses at St. Thomas' Hospital in London demonstrated the power of this approach. The school produced highly skilled nurses who were not only capable of providing excellent care but also of leading others and implementing new practices. These nurses went on to spread Florence's methods across the globe, establishing nursing schools and hospitals in other countries and bringing her ideas to the wider world.

But Florence's influence didn't stop at nursing education. She also revolutionized hospital design. During the Crimean War, she had seen firsthand how the physical environment of a hospital could impact patient outcomes. Overcrowded wards, poor ventilation, and unsanitary conditions all contributed to high rates of infection and death.

Florence was convinced that the design of a hospital was as important as the care provided within it.

She advocated for the construction of hospitals that were clean, well-ventilated, and organized to prevent the spread of disease. Florence introduced the concept of "pavilion-style" hospitals, which featured separate wings or pavilions for different types of patients. This design allowed for better air circulation and made it easier to control infections. The use of large windows, high ceilings, and wide corridors ensured that fresh air and natural light could flow through the wards, creating a healthier environment for patients and staff alike.

These design principles were revolutionary at the time, but they quickly became standard practice. Hospitals around the world began adopting Florence's ideas, leading to significant improvements in patient care. The emphasis on cleanliness and proper sanitation also laid the foundation for the development of antiseptic practices, which would later become a cornerstone of modern medicine.

Florence's work extended beyond the walls of hospitals, influencing public health on a broader scale. She was a pioneer in the use of statistics to analyze health outcomes and identify areas for improvement. During the Crimean War, Florence had meticulously recorded data on death rates, the causes of illness, and the effectiveness of different treatments. She used this data to advocate for changes that would save lives, both in military hospitals and in civilian healthcare systems.

One of her most famous contributions to public health was the development of the "polar area diagram," also known as the "Nightingale rose diagram." This innovative chart allowed Florence to visually represent the causes of death in military hospitals, highlighting the impact of preventable diseases. The diagram was a powerful tool in her campaign for healthcare reform, as it made the data accessible and easy to understand for policymakers and the general public.

Florence's use of statistics to drive healthcare improvements was groundbreaking, and it established a new standard for how health data should be collected and used. Her approach laid the groundwork for the field of epidemiology, the study of how diseases spread and can be controlled. Today, the use of data to inform public health decisions is a fundamental aspect of healthcare, and it all began with Florence's insistence on the importance of accurate, evidence-based information.

The impact of Florence's work can also be seen in the way she reshaped the role of nurses within the healthcare system. Before Florence, nurses were often seen as little more than helpers to doctors, with limited responsibilities and authority. Florence challenged this view by demonstrating that nurses could play a critical role in patient care, from managing wards to making decisions about treatment. She believed that nurses should be empowered to take on leadership roles and to advocate for their patients.

This shift in perspective helped to professionalize nursing and to establish it as a distinct and essential part of the healthcare system. Florence's emphasis on training and her belief in the value of skilled, compassionate care helped to elevate the status of nurses, giving them the respect and recognition they deserved. Today, nursing is recognized as a vital profession, and nurses are seen as key partners in the delivery of healthcare.

Florence's influence on healthcare wasn't limited to the United Kingdom. Her ideas and methods spread across Europe, North America, and beyond, inspiring a global movement to improve the quality of care. Nursing schools based on her model were established in countries around the world, and her principles of hospital design and public health were adopted by healthcare systems in many different contexts. Florence's work helped to create a more humane and effective approach to healthcare, one that recognized the importance of both the physical and emotional well-being of patients.

florence's awards and honors

Florence Nightingale's work in revolutionizing healthcare and nursing did not go unnoticed. While she never sought fame or recognition, her tireless efforts to improve the lives of others earned her numerous awards and honors throughout her life. These accolades were a testament to the profound impact she had on the world, not just in her own time but for generations to come. Among these honors, the establishment of the Nightingale Medal stands out as a symbol of her lasting legacy.

One of the earliest recognitions Florence received was the Order of Merit, which was awarded to her by King Edward VII in 1907. The Order of Merit was a highly prestigious honor, reserved for individuals who had made exceptional contributions to the arts, sciences, or public service. Florence was the first woman to receive this award, and it was a reflection of the extraordinary influence she had wielded in transforming healthcare. By this time, Florence was already well into her seventies and confined to her home due to illness, but the award highlighted the lasting impact of her work.

Florence's recognition wasn't limited to Britain. Her work had resonated around the world, and many countries sought to honor her contributions. The French government awarded her the Légion d'Honneur, one of the highest decorations in France. This award was particularly meaningful, as it acknowledged the international significance of her work in healthcare and nursing. Florence's influence had crossed borders, inspiring improvements in hospitals and nursing practices in countries far beyond her homeland.

Another important recognition was the Royal Red Cross, which was presented to Florence by Queen Victoria in 1883. The Royal Red Cross was established to recognize exceptional services in military nursing, and it was a fitting honor for Florence, whose work during the Crimean War had saved countless lives. The Queen herself had been deeply moved by the reports of Florence's dedication and compassion, and this award was a personal acknowledgment of the difference she had made.

But perhaps the most enduring symbol of Florence's legacy is the Nightingale Medal. Established in 1912 by the International Committee of the Red Cross (ICRC), the Nightingale Medal is awarded to nurses and nursing aides who have shown exceptional courage and devotion to the sick and injured. The medal is named in honor of Florence, and it serves as a lasting tribute to her pioneering work in nursing.

The Nightingale Medal is the highest international distinction a nurse can receive, and it embodies the values that Florence held dear—compassion, dedication, and a commitment to improving the lives of others. The medal is awarded every two years to a select group of nurses from around the world, and it recognizes not just their skill, but their willingness to go above and beyond in the service of humanity. In this way, the Nightingale Medal carries forward Florence's belief that nursing is not just a profession, but a calling.

The design of the Nightingale Medal is simple yet powerful. It features an image of Florence Nightingale on one side, holding her iconic lamp, a symbol of the light she brought into the lives of those she cared for. The reverse side bears the words "For devotion to humanity," capturing the essence of what the medal represents. Each recipient of the Nightingale Medal is chosen not just for their expertise in nursing, but for their embodiment of the qualities that Florence exemplified.

Florence herself never sought recognition for her work, and she was often uncomfortable with the attention she received. She preferred to focus on the work itself, always striving to find new ways to improve healthcare and to support those who needed it most. Yet the honors she received were not just about celebrating her achievements—they were about recognizing the transformative impact she had on the world and the lives she had touched through her compassion and dedication.

In addition to formal awards, Florence received countless letters of thanks and appreciation from people around the world. Patients, families, fellow nurses, and even government officials wrote to express their gratitude for the difference she had made. These letters were a reflection of the personal connections Florence had forged through her work, and they served as a reminder that her influence went far beyond the walls of hospitals and institutions.

6 /
florence
nightingale's legacy

florence's later years

AFTER THE CRIMEAN War and the subsequent recognition she received, Florence's health took a significant downturn. The long hours, the stress of her work, and the harsh conditions she endured during the war had left her physically weakened. She suffered from what was then referred to as "Crimean fever," likely a chronic form of brucellosis or a related illness, which left her bedridden for long periods. Despite her physical frailty, Florence's determination remained unshaken. She adapted to her new reality, finding ways to continue her work from the confines of her room.

One of the ways Florence stayed connected to her mission was through writing. Even though she could no longer travel or engage in hands-on nursing, she became a prolific writer on subjects related to healthcare, hospital management, and nursing education. Her room became a hub of activity, with papers, books, and letters scattered everywhere. She corresponded with government officials, hospital administrators, and fellow reformers, offering advice and advocating for improvements. Her writing wasn't just about sharing her knowledge—it was a way for her to continue shaping the future of healthcare, even from a distance.

Florence's most famous work, Notes on Nursing: What It Is and What It Is Not, was published in 1859, but she continued to expand and update her ideas throughout her later years. This book wasn't just for nurses; it was intended for anyone responsible for the care of others, including family members and caregivers. In it, Florence laid out the principles of good nursing, emphasizing the importance of cleanliness, fresh air, proper nutrition, and compassionate care. These ideas, though common sense today, were revolutionary at the time and had a profound impact on the way nursing was practiced.

Her influence also extended to the design and management of hospitals. Florence had long believed that the environment in which patients were treated played a critical role in their recovery. She worked tirelessly to promote the idea that hospitals should be designed with the patient's well-being in mind, advocating for better ventilation, sanitation, and organization. Even from her bed, Florence contributed to the planning of new hospitals, using her expertise to ensure that these facilities were built to the highest standards.

Florence's ability to influence public health policy was another testament to her enduring impact. She used her extensive knowledge and experience to advise governments on how to improve healthcare systems. For example, during the cholera outbreaks of the 1860s, Florence's guidance was instrumental in shaping public health responses. She argued for better sanitation, clean water supplies, and improved waste management —measures that were crucial in controlling the spread of the disease. Her work laid the foundation for modern public health practices and highlighted the importance of prevention in healthcare.

Florence's later years were also marked by her continued involvement in nursing education. The Nightingale Training School for Nurses, which she had founded at St. Thomas' Hospital in London, continued to thrive under her guidance. Although she could no longer teach in person, Florence remained closely connected to the school, mentoring the staff and providing direction on the curriculum. She believed that nursing education was the key to improving patient care, and she was committed to ensuring that the next generation of nurses was well-trained and prepared for the challenges they would face.

Florence's mentorship extended beyond the walls of her training school. She became a source of inspiration and guidance for nurses around the world. Many young nurses sought her advice, and Florence took the time to write letters of encouragement and share her insights. These correspondences were more than just professional advice; they were a way for Florence to pass on her values and her belief in the importance of compassionate care.

Even as her health continued to decline, Florence's impact on healthcare and nursing grew. Her ideas spread far beyond Britain, influencing the development of nursing education and hospital practices in countries around the world. Nurses trained in her methods went on to establish nursing schools and hospitals in places as far-flung as Australia, Canada, and India. Florence's principles of hygiene, organization, and patient-centered care became the foundation of modern nursing, ensuring that her legacy would endure long after she was gone.

Florence's later years were not without challenges. She struggled with the limitations imposed by her illness, often feeling frustrated by her inability to be more physically active in her work. Yet she never allowed these challenges to diminish her resolve. Florence's spirit remained indomitable, and she continued to find ways to contribute to the field she had dedicated her life to. Her resilience in the face of adversity was a powerful example to others, showing that even when physical strength fades, the power of the mind and the heart can continue to make a difference.

Florence Nightingale's later years were a testament to her unwavering dedication to healthcare and nursing. Even as her body weakened, her influence only grew stronger. Through her writing, her mentorship, and her ongoing involvement in public health and nursing education, Florence continued to shape the future of healthcare. Her life's work was far from over, and her contributions during this period laid the groundwork for many of the advancements in healthcare that we take for granted today.

the florence nightingale effect

Florence's approach to nursing was ground-breaking because it emphasized the importance of compassion and scientific rigor. Before she entered the scene, nursing was seen as unskilled labor, something that didn't require much training or education. Hospitals were often dirty and chaotic, and the people who worked there were expected to follow orders rather than think critically about patient care. Florence changed all of that. She insisted that nursing was a profession that required both heart and mind—a combination of empathy, compassion, and rigorous attention to detail.

One of the most significant ways Florence's work continues to influence nursing is through the emphasis on education. Today, nursing schools around the world are built on the principles she established: that nurses must be well-trained, knowledgeable, and prepared to take on complex medical challenges. The curriculum she developed for the Nightingale Training School for Nurses laid the foundation for modern nursing education, with a focus on hands-on experience, scientific knowl-edge, and ethical care.

The "Florence Nightingale Effect" can also be seen in the way hospitals are designed and run.

Florence was one of the first to recognize the importance of the environment in patient recovery. She argued that hospitals should be places of healing, not just treatment. This meant creating spaces that were clean, well-lit, and designed with the patient's comfort and well-being in mind. The idea that the physical environment can impact health outcomes is now a fundamental principle in healthcare design, thanks to Florence's pioneering work.

The influence of Florence Nightingale extends beyond just the field of nursing. Her use of statistics and data to drive healthcare improvements was revolutionary. During the Crimean War, she meticulously gathered data on patient outcomes, using it to demonstrate the effectiveness of her methods and to advocate for changes in military and civilian hospitals. Her work in this area laid the groundwork for modern epidemiology and public health, fields that rely on data to understand and address health issues on a large scale.

Florence's insistence on using data to inform decisions has become a cornerstone of evidence-based practice, a concept that is now fundamental in healthcare. Evidence-based practice involves making clinical decisions based on the best available research, clinical expertise, and patient preferences. This approach ensures that patient care is grounded in scientific evidence, leading to better outcomes. Florence's early work in this area was a precursor to the sophisticated data-driven healthcare systems we have today.

The "Florence Nightingale Effect" also refers to the way she elevated the role of nurses within the healthcare system. Before Florence, nurses were often seen as little more than assistants to doctors. They were expected to follow orders without question and had little authority or autonomy. Florence changed this by demonstrating that nurses had a critical role to play in patient care. She showed that nurses were not just caregivers but also advocates for their patients, with the knowledge and skills to make important decisions about care.

This shift in perception helped to professionalize nursing and to establish it as a respected career. Today, nurses are recognized as essential members of the healthcare team, with their own areas of expertise and responsibility. They are involved in every aspect of patient care, from diagnosis and treatment to recovery and rehabilitation. Florence's work laid the foundation for this transformation, ensuring that nurses are valued for the vital contributions they make to healthcare.

Another lasting impact of Florence's work is the emphasis on patient-centered care. Florence believed that healthcare should be focused on the needs and well-being of the patient, rather than just treating the illness. She understood that patients are individuals with their own experiences, fears, and needs, and that care should be tailored to each person's unique situation. This approach to care has become a guiding principle in modern healthcare, influencing everything from how hospitals are designed to how medical professionals are trained.

The "Florence Nightingale Effect" is also evident in the global reach of her influence. Florence's principles of nursing and healthcare were not confined to Britain; they spread around the world. Her methods were adopted by healthcare systems in Europe, North America, Asia, and beyond, leading to significant improvements in patient care across the globe. Nurses trained in her methods went on to establish nursing schools and hospitals in other countries, spreading her ideas and practices far and wide.

Florence's work also paved the way for the development of nursing as a research-based profession. Today, nursing research is a vital part of the healthcare field, with nurses conducting studies on everything from patient care techniques to healthcare policy. This focus on research ensures that nursing practice continues to evolve and improve, driven by new knowledge and insights. Florence's early work in collecting and analyzing data was a precursor to this research-driven approach, demonstrating the importance of evidence in improving care.

7 /

fun facts about florence

ONE OF THE more surprising facts about Florence is that she was an early data scientist, long before that term even existed. Florence had a deep love for mathematics, something that was unusual for women of her time. She was particularly skilled in statistics, and she used this knowledge to analyze healthcare data, helping to drive her reforms. Florence even invented a type of pie chart called the "polar area diagram" to illustrate the causes of death in military hospitals. This innovation wasn't just a tool for her own work; it became an important way to communicate complex ideas in a simple, visual format, making data accessible to policymakers and the public.

Beyond her love for numbers, Florence was also a passionate writer. She wrote extensively throughout her life, not only about nursing and healthcare but also about a wide range of other topics, including religion, philosophy, and women's rights. Florence kept journals, wrote letters, and published books, using her writing as a way to process her thoughts and share her ideas with the world. Her book Notes on Nursing became a cornerstone of nursing education, but she also penned works that delved into her personal beliefs and experiences. Writing was more than just a tool for advocacy—it was a way for Florence to connect with others and express her inner world.

Florence's love for animals is another aspect of her life that many people might not know about. She had a special fondness for owls, and one owl in particular became her beloved pet. Florence found the small, injured owl in Athens, Greece, while she was traveling with her family. She named the owl Athena, after the Greek goddess of wisdom, and nursed it back to health. Athena became a constant companion to Florence, even traveling with her back to England. The owl would perch on Florence's shoulder as she wrote or worked, becoming a comforting presence in her life. Florence's compassion for animals mirrored her compassion for people, and she treated all living beings with care and kindness.

Despite her serious demeanor in public, Florence had a quirky side that came out in her daily life. She was known for her meticulous habits, particularly when it came to cleanliness and organization. Florence was almost obsessive about keeping her environment tidy, and she believed that a clean and orderly space was essential for clear thinking and good health. This attention to detail was something she carried into her work in hospitals, where she insisted on the highest standards of cleanliness to prevent the spread of disease.

Florence also had a curious mind and a love for learning that extended far beyond healthcare. She was deeply interested in languages and was fluent in several, including French, Italian, and German. She used her language skills to read texts in their original languages, which allowed her to engage with ideas and cultures from around the world. This intellectual curiosity was a driving force in her life, pushing her to constantly seek out new knowledge and perspectives.

Another little-known fact about Florence is that she had a complex relationship with fame. While she was widely celebrated for her work, she was uncomfortable with the attention it brought her. Florence was a deeply private person who valued her solitude and often felt overwhelmed by the public's fascination with her. She would sometimes retreat from public life, preferring the quiet of her home to the spotlight. Despite this, she recognized the power of her public image and used it to further her causes, even if it meant stepping outside of her comfort zone.

Florence's dedication to her work often came at a personal cost. She was a workaholic, driven by a sense of duty that sometimes bordered on obsession. This relentless focus on her mission led her to push herself to the brink of exhaustion, and she often struggled with her health as a result. Florence suffered from chronic illness for much of her life, likely due to the physical and emotional toll of her work during the Crimean War. Despite her health challenges, she continued to work tirelessly, driven by an unwavering commitment to improving healthcare.

One of the more charming quirks of Florence's personality was her love for tea. Like many Brits of her time, Florence was an avid tea drinker, and she believed that a good cup of tea could solve almost any problem. She would often take breaks from her work to enjoy a quiet moment with her tea, using the time to relax and gather her thoughts. Tea was more than just a beverage for Florence—it was a small ritual that brought a sense of calm and comfort to her hectic life.

Florence also had a strong sense of humor, which she used to cope with the stresses of her work. She was known to make witty remarks and often used humor to lighten the mood, even in the most serious situations. This playful side of her personality was a way for Florence to stay grounded and connected to the people around her, reminding everyone that even in the most challenging times, there's always room for a bit of laughter.

8 /
activities

ONE OF THE simplest yet most impactful projects that children can undertake is creating their own first-aid kit. A first-aid kit is more than just a collection of bandages and ointments; it's a tool for helping others in times of need. By assembling a kit, children can learn about the different items used in basic first aid and how they can be applied in real-life situations. This activity also fosters a sense of responsibility and preparedness, key qualities that Florence Nightingale herself would have championed.

To start, gather the materials needed for the first-aid kit. You can use a small, sturdy box or a plastic container as the base. Encourage children to decorate their kits with stickers, markers, or paint to make them feel more personal and engaging. This part of the activity allows for creativity and helps children take ownership of their kits.

Next, discuss the importance of each item in the first-aid kit and how it might be used. Bandages, for example, are used to protect cuts and scrapes, while antiseptic wipes help clean wounds to prevent infection. Talk about how each item contributes to the overall goal of providing care and comfort to someone who is hurt.

Here's a list of items that can be included in a simple first-aid kit:

- Adhesive bandages (various sizes)
    - Sterile gauze pads
    - Adhesive tape
    - Antiseptic wipes
    - Tweezers
    - Scissors (safety scissors for younger children)
    - Cotton balls or swabs

- An ice pack (a reusable one that can be stored in a freezer)
- A small flashlight
- A pair of disposable gloves
- A notepad and pencil (to write down any important information, such as allergies or the time of an injury)

As children place each item into their kits, explain how and when it might be used. For example, you could demonstrate how to apply a bandage to a pretend cut, or show how to use the tweezers to remove a splinter. This hands-on learning helps children understand the practical application of each item and reinforces the importance of being prepared.

Once the kits are assembled, encourage children to practice using them in a safe, supervised environment. You can set up a few simple scenarios, such as treating a scraped knee or applying a cold pack to a bump. These role-playing exercises not only reinforce the skills they've learned but also build confidence in their ability to respond to minor injuries.

. . .

Another great way to engage children in hands-on learning is through basic hygiene activities, such as practicing proper handwashing techniques. Florence Nightingale was a strong advocate for cleanliness, recognizing its vital role in preventing the spread of disease. Teaching children about the importance of hand hygiene is a simple yet effective way to instill healthy habits.

To make this activity more interactive, create a "germ simulation" using a bit of glitter or washable paint. Place a small amount on a child's hand and explain that it represents germs. Then, have them try to wash the glitter or paint off using water alone. They'll quickly see that it doesn't come off easily. Next, add soap and demonstrate the proper way to wash hands—scrubbing all parts of the hands, including between the fingers and under the nails, for at least 20 seconds. After they've washed their hands with soap, they'll notice that the "germs" come off much more effectively. This visual and tactile experience reinforces the importance of thorough handwashing.

. . .

In addition to first-aid kits and hygiene activities, another hands-on learning project involves creating "comfort packs" for people in need. Florence Nightingale was known for her compassion, and this activity is a wonderful way to teach children about empathy and the importance of helping others.

A comfort pack is a small bag or box filled with items that can bring comfort to someone going through a difficult time. These packs can be donated to hospitals, shelters, or anyone in the community who might need a little extra care. Encourage children to think about what items might be comforting—things like a soft blanket, a small stuffed animal, a notebook and pen, or a book of uplifting stories.

As children assemble their comfort packs, talk with them about the importance of kindness and how even small gestures can make a big difference in someone's life. This activity not only teaches practical skills but also fosters a sense of empathy and social responsibility.

. . .

For those interested in learning more about the medical field, a basic introduction to vital signs can be an engaging hands-on activity. Teach children how to take a pulse, either on themselves or on a partner. You can explain that the pulse is the heartbeat felt through the walls of the arteries and that it's an important indicator of health.

To take a pulse, have the child place two fingers (not the thumb) on the wrist, just below the base of the thumb, or on the side of the neck. Show them how to count the beats for 30 seconds and then double that number to get the beats per minute. This simple exercise introduces children to the concept of vital signs and helps them understand one of the basic ways that healthcare providers assess a person's health.

Another vital sign to explore is temperature. If you have a digital thermometer, you can show children how to use it to take their own temperature. Explain that body temperature can tell us a lot about how we're feeling and that it's an important tool doctors use to determine if someone might be sick.

discussion questions

What does compassion mean to you, and how can you show it to others?

Florence Nightingale's compassion was a driving force in her life, leading her to care for soldiers, reform healthcare, and advocate for better treatment of the sick. Asking children to reflect on what compassion means in their own lives can help them identify ways to practice kindness and empathy. Encourage them to think about situations where they've shown compassion or where they might have missed an opportunity to help someone. Discuss how small acts of kindness, like helping a friend or being understanding towards others, can have a big impact.

How do you think Florence felt when she decided to become a nurse, even though it wasn't a common job for women at the time?

Florence faced significant societal pressure to conform to traditional roles for women, yet she chose a path that was unconventional and challenging. This question invites children to put themselves in Florence's shoes and consider how they might feel if they were pursuing something that others didn't understand or support. Discuss the importance of following one's passions and the courage it takes to go against the grain. This can lead to a broader conversation about how to handle peer pressure or societal expectations in their own lives.

Why do you think hard work was important to Florence, and how can hard work help you achieve your goals?

Florence Nightingale's success was not just the result of her intelligence or compassion—it was also due to her incredible work ethic. By discussing the value of hard work, children can begin to understand that achieving goals often requires effort, persistence, and dedication. Ask them to think about a time when they worked hard to accomplish something, whether it was learning a new skill, completing a project, or helping someone else. Explore how they felt during the process and how they felt once they achieved their goal, reinforcing the idea that hard work is a key ingredient in success.

· · ·

How did Florence's determination help her overcome challenges, and what challenges have you faced that required determination?

Florence encountered numerous obstacles throughout her life, from opposition to her ideas to physical illness. Her determination allowed her to push through these challenges and make a lasting impact. Encourage children to think about their own challenges—whether at school, in friendships, or in pursuing a personal goal—and how determination helped them overcome those challenges. This discussion can help them see that persistence in the face of difficulties is a valuable trait that can lead to personal growth and achievement.

What are some ways you can help others in your community, just like Florence helped the soldiers and the sick?

Florence Nightingale's life was dedicated to helping others, and her legacy is a reminder of the importance of service. Ask children to brainstorm ways they can make a difference in their own communities, whether through volunteer work, acts of kindness, or supporting a cause they care about. Discuss how even small actions, like helping a neighbor or participating in a community project, can contribute to the well-being of others and create a positive impact. This question encourages children to think about the role they can play in their community and how they can be agents of change.

How did Florence's work change the way we think about nursing and healthcare today?

Florence Nightingale revolutionized nursing and healthcare, laying the foundation for modern practices. This question encourages children to think about how her work has influenced the world we live in today. Discuss the differences between healthcare during Florence's time and now, and how her innovations in hygiene, hospital design, and nursing education have shaped current practices. This can also lead to a conversation about the importance of learning from history and building on the work of those who came before us.

How can you use what you've learned from Florence's life to overcome your own fears or doubts?

Florence was not immune to fear or doubt, but she didn't let these feelings stop her from pursuing her goals. By asking children to reflect on their own fears or doubts, you can help them identify strategies for overcoming these obstacles. Discuss how Florence might have felt when facing challenges and how she chose to move forward despite her fears. Encourage children to think about times when they've felt afraid or unsure and how they can draw on Florence's example to find the courage to keep going.

If you could ask Florence Nightingale one question, what would it be, and why?

This question invites children to engage their imaginations and connect personally with Florence's story. It encourages them to think deeply about what they admire or are curious about in her life. Whether they're interested in her thoughts on a particular event, her motivations, or her feelings during a challenging time, this question opens up a space for children to explore their own interests and curiosities. It also provides an opportunity for further research and learning, as they might seek out answers or discuss potential responses.

. . .

How can we apply Florence's values in our school or classroom environment?

Florence's values of compassion, hard work, and determination can be applied in many areas of life, including in school. Ask children to consider how these values can create a positive and supportive learning environment. Discuss ways they can show compassion to classmates, work hard in their studies, and stay determined when facing academic challenges. This conversation can help foster a sense of community and shared responsibility, reinforcing the idea that everyone plays a role in creating a positive and productive atmosphere.

What do you think Florence would say about the importance of teamwork, and how can we practice good teamwork in our activities?

Florence Nightingale understood the importance of teamwork in achieving her goals, whether it was working with other nurses or collaborating with doctors and hospital administrators. This question encourages children to reflect on the role of teamwork in their own lives. Discuss the qualities that make a good team member, such as communication, cooperation, and respect for others' ideas. Explore how these qualities can be practiced in group projects, sports, or other activities. By understanding the value of teamwork, children can learn to work more effectively with others and appreciate the collective effort needed to achieve common goals.

These discussion questions are designed to inspire thoughtful conversations between children, parents, and teachers. They provide a platform for exploring Florence Nightingale's life and legacy in a way that is both personal and relevant, encouraging children to think about how they can apply her values in their own lives. Through these discussions, children can gain a deeper understanding of Florence's impact and how her principles of compassion, hard work, and determination can guide them in their own journeys.

9 /
glossary and resources

glossary of terms

CRIMEAN WAR

The Crimean War was a conflict fought from 1853 to 1856 between Russia and an alliance of Britain, France, the Ottoman Empire, and Sardinia. The war was primarily over control of territories in the Ottoman Empire and access to important trade routes. The Crimean War is significant in the story of Florence Nightingale because it was during this conflict that she became famous for her work in improving the conditions in military hospitals and caring for wounded soldiers. Her efforts during the war laid the foundation for modern nursing.

. . .

Nurse

A nurse is a healthcare professional who cares for people who are sick, injured, or otherwise in need of medical assistance. Nurses work in various settings, including hospitals, clinics, and schools, and they perform a wide range of tasks, from administering medication to providing emotional support. Florence Nightingale is often credited with establishing nursing as a respected and professional career, emphasizing the importance of education, hygiene, and compassionate care.

Hygiene

Hygiene refers to practices that promote health and prevent the spread of disease, particularly through cleanliness. Florence Nightingale was a strong advocate for hygiene in hospitals, recognizing that clean environments were essential for preventing infections and improving patient outcomes. Her emphasis on hygiene revolutionized the way hospitals were run and helped to reduce the high rates of illness and death in medical facilities.

• • •

Sanitation

Sanitation involves the systems and practices that ensure cleanliness and the safe disposal of waste, particularly human waste. During the Crimean War, Florence Nightingale identified poor sanitation as a major cause of disease among soldiers. She implemented measures to improve sanitation in the hospitals where she worked, such as better waste disposal and clean water supplies. These efforts helped to reduce the spread of disease and set new standards for hospital management.

Infection

An infection occurs when harmful bacteria, viruses, or other microorganisms enter the body and cause illness. During the Crimean War, infections were a leading cause of death among soldiers, often due to unsanitary conditions in hospitals. Florence Nightingale's work in improving hygiene and sanitation played a crucial role in reducing infections and saving lives. Her understanding of the importance of preventing infection was ahead of her time and laid the groundwork for modern infection control practices.

. . .

Triage

Triage is the process of determining the priority of patients' treatments based on the severity of their condition. This practice is particularly important in emergency situations where resources are limited, such as during a war. While the concept of triage existed before Florence Nightingale's time, her work in organizing and managing military hospitals during the Crimean War helped to develop more systematic approaches to patient care, including the prioritization of those most in need.

Hospital Ward

A hospital ward is a large room or area in a hospital where patients with similar medical needs are cared for. Wards are often organized by type of illness or injury, allowing for more efficient care. Florence Nightingale introduced the idea of organizing hospital wards to improve patient outcomes, ensuring that patients received the appropriate care and that the risk of infection was minimized.

St. Thomas' Hospital

St. Thomas' Hospital is a large teaching hospital in London, England. It is historically significant because it was the location of the Nightingale Training School for Nurses, which Florence Nightingale founded in 1860. The school was one of the first to offer formal training for nurses and set the standards for nursing education worldwide. St. Thomas' Hospital remains an important institution in the field of healthcare and nursing education.

Nightingale Training School for Nurses

The Nightingale Training School for Nurses was the first professional nursing school, established by Florence Nightingale at St. Thomas' Hospital in London. The school focused on providing rigorous training for nurses, emphasizing both practical skills and theoretical knowledge. Graduates of the school went on to spread Florence's principles of nursing across the world, helping to establish nursing as a respected and essential profession.

The Lady with the Lamp

"The Lady with the Lamp" is a nickname given

to Florence Nightingale by the soldiers she cared for during the Crimean War. The name comes from her habit of making nightly rounds through the hospital wards, checking on her patients while carrying a small lamp. This image of Florence with her lamp became a symbol of her compassion and dedication, and it remains one of the most enduring representations of her legacy.

Florence Nightingale Medal

The Florence Nightingale Medal is the highest international distinction awarded to nurses or nursing aides who have shown exceptional courage and devotion to caring for the sick and wounded. Established by the International Committee of the Red Cross (ICRC) in 1912, the medal honors those who embody the values and principles that Florence Nightingale stood for. The recipients of this award are recognized for their outstanding contributions to healthcare and humanitarian work.

Statistics

Statistics is the branch of mathematics that deals with the collection, analysis, interpretation, and presentation of numerical data. Florence Nightingale was one of the first people to use statistics to improve healthcare, analyzing data from military hospitals to demonstrate the need for better sanitation and hygiene. Her use of statistics to advocate for healthcare reform was groundbreaking and helped to establish the importance of evidence-based practice in medicine.

Polar Area Diagram

The polar area diagram is a type of chart that Florence Nightingale invented to visually represent data, particularly the causes of death in military hospitals during the Crimean War. The diagram, which is a variation of a pie chart, made it easier for people to understand the impact of poor hygiene and sanitation on soldier mortality. Florence's use of the polar area diagram was an early example of data visualization, a technique that is now widely used in many fields to present complex information in a clear and accessible way.

Compassion

Compassion is the ability to understand and empathize with the suffering of others, and to take action to help alleviate that suffering. Florence

Nightingale's compassion for the sick and wounded was a driving force behind her work, motivating her to improve conditions in hospitals and to advocate for better healthcare for all. Compassion remains a core value in nursing and healthcare, guiding professionals in their care for patients.

Determination

Determination is the quality of being resolute and committed to achieving a goal, even in the face of obstacles or challenges. Florence Nightingale's determination to improve healthcare and nursing, despite the many barriers she faced, was a key factor in her success. Her determination continues to inspire people around the world to pursue their goals with perseverance and courage.

Hygiene Hypothesis

The hygiene hypothesis is a scientific theory that suggests that a lack of exposure to certain microorganisms in early childhood can lead to a higher susceptibility to allergies and autoimmune diseases. While this concept was developed long after

Florence Nightingale's time, her work in promoting hygiene and cleanliness in healthcare settings was a precursor to the modern understanding of the role of microorganisms in health and disease.

Scutari

Scutari, now known as Üsküdar, is a district in Istanbul, Turkey. During the Crimean War, it was the site of a major British military hospital where Florence Nightingale worked. The hospital at Scutari was where Florence made many of her most significant contributions to nursing and healthcare, transforming it from a place of despair into a more organized and sanitary environment that saved countless lives.

Pavilion Hospital

A pavilion hospital is a type of hospital design that consists of separate buildings or wings, each with its own specialized function, such as wards for different types of patients. Florence Nightingale advocated for the pavilion design as a way to improve ventilation, reduce the spread of infection, and provide better care for patients. This design became widely adopted in the construction of modern hospitals.

Public Health

Public health is the science and practice of protecting and improving the health of populations through the prevention and control of diseases, the promotion of healthy behaviors, and the development of policies that support health. Florence Nightingale's work laid the foundation for many aspects of modern public health, particularly her emphasis on hygiene, sanitation, and the use of data to inform healthcare decisions.

resources

Websites and Online Resources

1.   The   Florence   Nightingale   Museum (www.florence-nightingale.co.uk)

The Florence Nightingale Museum, located in London, offers a wealth of information about Florence's life and legacy. The museum's website features virtual exhibits, educational resources, and interactive content that bring Florence's story to life. Visitors can explore the museum's collections, learn about key events in Florence's life, and even take a virtual tour of the museum.

2. The British Library's Florence Nightingale Collection (www.bl.uk)

The British Library houses an extensive collection of Florence Nightingale's letters, papers, and other personal documents. Their online collection allows visitors to explore these materials, providing a unique glimpse into Florence's thoughts, experiences, and correspondence. This resource is particularly valuable for those interested in primary sources and original documents related to Florence Nightingale.

3. Nightingale Society (www.nightingalesociety.com)

The Nightingale Society is dedicated to preserving and promoting the legacy of Florence Nightingale. Their website offers articles, research papers, and resources on various aspects of Florence's life and work. It's a great place to find in-depth information and connect with a community of people who share an interest in

Florence Nightingale and her contributions to nursing.

4. The Wellcome Collection (www.wellcomecollection.org)

The Wellcome Collection, based in London, is a museum and library that explores the connections between medicine, life, and art. Their website features a wide range of resources related to the history of healthcare, including materials on Florence Nightingale. The Wellcome Collection's digital archives include photographs, documents, and artifacts that provide a richer understanding of Florence's world.

5. HistoryExtra's Florence Nightingale Articles (www.historyextra.com)

HistoryExtra, the website of BBC History Magazine, offers a variety of articles and features on Florence Nightingale. These pieces cover different aspects of her life, from her role in the Crimean War to her influence on public health. The site is a good resource for those looking to read accessible, well-researched content on Florence and other historical figures.

.   .   .

Further Exploration of Nursing and Healthcare

"The American Nurse Project" (www.american-nurseproject.com)

The American Nurse Project is a multimedia initiative that celebrates the work of nurses across the United States. The project includes a documentary film, a book, and a website featuring stories and portraits of nurses. It's an inspiring resource that highlights the diversity and dedication of the nursing profession, connecting modern-day nurses with the values Florence Nightingale championed.

The National Institute of Nursing Research (www.ninr.nih.gov)

The National Institute of Nursing Research (NINR) is part of the U.S. National Institutes of Health (NIH) and supports research to improve the health and well-being of individuals, families, and communities. Their website offers information on the latest nursing research, resources for aspiring nurses, and educational materials that explore the impact of nursing on public health.

.   .   .

Nursing Times (www.nursingtimes.net)

Nursing Times is a leading source of news, analysis, and opinion in the nursing profession. Their website provides articles on a wide range of topics related to nursing, including clinical practice, healthcare policy, and professional development. It's a valuable resource for anyone interested in staying up-to-date with the latest developments in nursing and healthcare.